THE ABCS OF
LOVE AND SEX

© 2017 Gina Ogden, PhD, LMFT

All rights reserved.
No part of this book may be reproduced
in any form whatsoever without permission in writing from the
publisher, except for use in articles and reviews.

Proceeds from book sales will be donated to the
Center for Spiritual Living in Carlsbad, CA, which
Jane Claypool founded, and sustained for many years.

Published by

PO Box 400443
Cambridge, MA 02140

Library of Congress Cataloging-in-Publication Data
applied for

ISBN: 978-0-9672705-1-7

TO THE WISE WOMEN AND COURAGEOUS MEN WHO ARE LEARNING TO EXPAND THE ALPHABET OF LOVE AND SEXUAL INTIMACY

OPENING WORDS

What's a four-letter word that means great sex?

According to many sex educators it's T-A-L-K, the fine art of sexual communication. For it's in expressing our likes and dislikes and in listening sensitively to our partners, that the most intimate connections are conceived and born.

As a long-time sexuality therapist and researcher, it's been my experience that such communication involves all of us – body, mind, heart, and spirit.

So the intent of this seemingly simple ABC book is to awaken every one of our senses to the multiple possibilities inherent in our most intimate relationships, and to invite new communication skills by offering a wide range of sexual issues to think about, feel into, and talk about.

The ABCs of Love and Sex is based on truths of current research, along with decades of clinical observation and personal experience. What's most important about this book, however, is that you use it as a launching pad for your own experiences and truths, so that it holds personal meaning for you.

I hope you'll use the images, narratives, and questions to help you explore nuances of love and sex in your own words, whether you blog, write in your journal, talk with your friends, or live these nuances with your partners—and your self.

A note on the art: For many years, I have loved the joyous drawings of my dear friend Jane Claypool—and it is my pleasure that we have been able to collaborate in print with one another at last.

Gina Ogden, PhD, LMFT
Cambridge, Massachusetts

A is for Adventure

Welcome to the roller-coaster journey of love and sex. It doesn't always turn out to be what we think it's going to be. Yet from the seeming chaos of our lives often emerges such exquisite sensitivity that our spirit of adventure expands long beyond physical lovemaking.

- What kind of sexual adventure are you on?
- What kind of sexual adventure would you like to be on?

Other A-words to consider: Alive, Affirmation, Awe, Acceptance, Allure, Altruism, Ask, Allow, Attention, Action, Appetite, Amorous, Arms, Aphrodisiac, Aphrodite—Goddess of Love.

A-words you'd like to add:

_____

_____

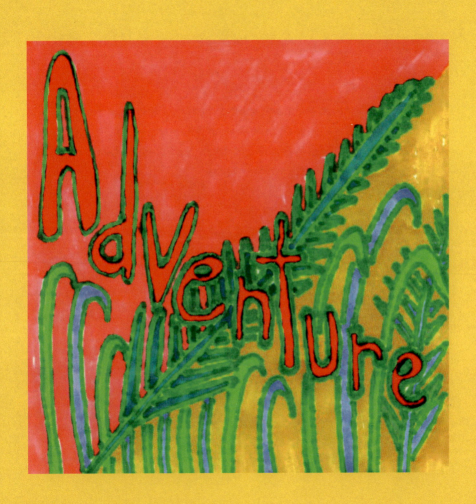

B IS FOR BLISS

When body, heart, mind, and spirit come together in sexual love and intimacy, we enter an over-the-rainbow state—a kind of high-definition Oz, where everything is vibrantly colored, and life seems effortless and filled with synchronicities.

- What does bliss feel like for you?
- How do you follow your bliss?

Other B-words to consider: Body, Beauty, Bold, Breasts, Beliefs, Bisexual, Butch, Bodacious, Balls, Belly, Bum, Bonding, Bondage, Bra, Boundaries, Breath, Breathing together, Bathing together.

B-words you'd like to add:

_____

_____

C IS FOR CONNECTION

Thousands of women and men report that true eroticism resides in relationship. It's about connection with our intimate partners—but first it's about the connections we develop with ourselves: body, mind, heart, and spirit. Because this is the relationship we have with us our whole lives long.

- How do you connect with yourself?
- How do you connect with your partner(s)?

Other C-words to consider: Caring, Confidence, Creativity, Choice, Comfort, Clitoris, Compassion, Cosmic, Contact, Conquest, Cuddle, Condom, Cute, Consensual, Curiosity, Courage.

C-words you'd like to add:

_____

_____

D IS FOR DARE

Have you ever wondered, "Isn't there something more to sex than just intercourse?" Yes, there is. Great sex is more than performance. It's about imagining and feeling what you want, and having the courage to try—as long as it's consensual and doesn't harm anyone, including yourself.

- What feels to you like unexplored territory in the realms of love, sex, and intimacy?
- What's the next daring step you're willing to take?

Other D-words to consider: Desire, Dream, Diversity, Dancing, Dirty dancing, Discernment, Dildo, Date, Dress up, Drag, Delicious, Delectable, Divine.

D-words you'd like to add:

_____

_____

E IS FOR ECSTASY

"To hell with happiness—I want ecstasy!"
This is what one bodacious woman said about sexual experiences that took her into cosmic realms. She also said it was really hard to talk about ecstasy-because so few people understood. So know that you're not alone if you can't find the right words to express the heights of sexual ecstasy.

- In a moment of sexual ecstasy have you ever experienced God, or a power greater than yourself?
- Who have you talked with about it?

Other E-words to consider: Emotion, Elation, Excitement, Edgy, Entertainment, Encouragement, Exploration, Eye-contact, Enfolding, Ejaculation, Energy, Eros, Eat, Ease, Easy.

E-words you'd like to add:

_____

_____

F IS FOR FUN

As a sex therapist I'm all for expanding definitions of sex beyond performance—that is, beyond just "doing it" with a goal of orgasm and maybe not much more. And I'm especially in favor of putting the FUN back into the notion of "sexual FUNction."

- What's something sexy you'd like to do for fun?
- Is that with or without a partner?

Other F-words to consider: Female, Femme, Flirt, Fantasy, Furry, Foot, Food, Fetish, Feeling, Fear, Fluid, Fresh, Funny, Freedom, Flying, Flow, Fellatio, Fidelity, Foreplay, Fairplay.

F-words you'd like to add:

_____

_____

G IS FOR GIFT

The most precious gifts are those that come from the essence of our being--like offerings to a beloved deity. These are the ones that require no thanks, only acceptance and joy.

- What's most precious to you about love and sexuality?
- What's an offering you can make on the altar of love and sensuality?

Other G-words to consider: Gender, Genital, Gentle, G-spot, G-string, Gay, Generous, Grace, Generative, Goddess, God, Gratitude, Gratify, Good, Grrrrrrrr.

G-words you'd like to add:

_____

_____

H IS FOR HEART

Almost four centuries ago, the French philosopher Blaise Pascal wrote that the heart has its reasons that are beyond all reasoning. Modern science tells us that the heart actually has its own intelligence. Have you ever noticed that the longest journey in the world seems to be the one we take from the head to the heart?

- What—or who—touches your heart?
- How do you follow your heart's reasons?

Other H-words to consider: Hug, Hormones, Honey, Honeymoon, Honesty, Heterosexual, Happiness, Hair, Humor, Heat, Hot, Healing, Holy, Horny, Humor, Hump, Her, Him.

H-words you'd like to add:

_____

_____

I IS FOR IMAGINATION

The brain is our most important sex organ, say informed sexologists. It's not all about the call of the genitals, it's also about releasing ourselves from the cultural trance that dictates how sex ought to be expressed. What's OK, what's not OK? What feels good, what doesn't feel good? What's the difference between a dream and a fantasy? The sky's the limit.

- What are your dreams and fantasies?
- Can you imagine yourself in the sky?

Other I-words to consider: I, Information, Invitation, Intuition, Inspiration, Intelligence, Intimacy, Incense, In love, Ignite, Intersex, Isis—Initiator into the Sexual Mysteries.

I-words you'd like to add:

_____

_____

J IS FOR JOY

When people speak about joy, three concepts stand out: connection, meaning, and transformation. These occur when we allow ourselves to be fully present. Breathe the joy. Feel it. Believe it. One woman said, "Connecting sex and spirit is powerful enough to manifest joy through me and bring me to my knees at the same time."

- What makes you jump for joy?
- What kinds of joy make you want to kneel?

Other J-words to consider: Journey, Juicy, Jewel, Jealousy, Jazzy, Judgment, Ju Ju.

J-words you'd like to add:

_____

_____

K IS FOR KINKY

One person's "kink" may be another's "vanilla." The trick for all of us is to know what we want—and to approach our individual preferences with open curiosity rather than automatic judgments.

- What feels way out there for you about love and sex?
- What are you most curious about?

Other K-words to consider: Kisses, Karma, Kindness, Kindred, Karezza, Knowing, Kneeling, Kegel exercises.

K-words you'd like to add:

_____

_____

L IS FOR LOVE

Love has a thousand faces—from heart-opening to heartbreaking. Is love necessary for great sex? Countless people say no. And countless more can't imagine sex without it: "We don't just have sex, we make love!"

- What's it like to be in love?
- What's it like to heal a broken heart?

Other L-words to consider: Lust, Listen, Light, Luminous, Liminal, Luscious, Lurid, Loose, Lyric, Lubrication, Laughter, Lesbian, Longing, Lips, Labia, Licking, Letting go, Liberation.

L-words you'd like to add:

_____

_____

M IS FOR MYSTERY

Sexual experience is one of the greatest mystery stories ever told—lush with emotion and sensation, a process of potential shipwreck on the shores of joy. Poets and scientists agree that how we navigate the mysteries of love and sex is a journey of continual discovery and awe.

- What mysteries do you want to explore?
- Have you ever been shipwrecked?

Other M-words to consider: Mystical, Music, Magnetic, Mirror, Magnificent, Marriage, Monogamy, Male, Masturbation, Meditation, Massage, Melt, Memory, Movement, Mindfulness, Me, More.

M-words you'd like to add:

_____

_____

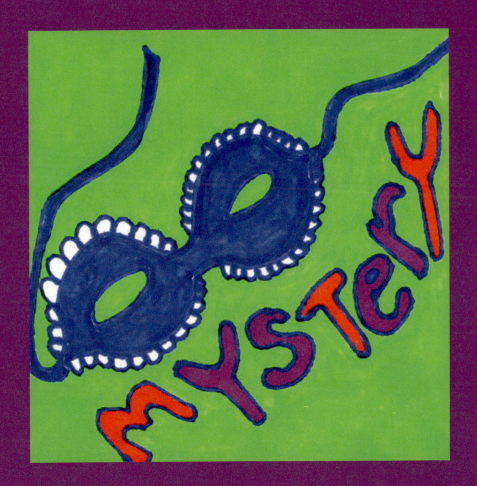

N IS FOR NAUGHTY

"Naughty" usually means breaking the rules other people have made. So many rules have accrued to sex over the centuries that almost anything fun we want to try becomes naughty.

- What's something naughty you'd like to try?
- Who would you like to try it with?

Other N-words to consider: New, Nurturing, Nuzzle, Negligee, Noise, Novel, Novice, Nuance, Nudity, Normal, Nice, Nipple, Nibble, Nervous, No, No-No.

N-words you'd like to add:

_____

_____

O IS FOR OPEN

Opening to the complexity of love and sex can shake loose our inner barriers and unlock our emotional doors. When we open up, our hearts melt along with our bodies. Anticipation and excitement meet deep-seated longing. Joy, delight, and surprise hold hands with passion and compassion.

- What are the keys to your body, mind, heart, and soul?
- What melts you?

Other O-words to consider: Oneness, Only, Orientation, On top, Oral, Orgy, Orgasm, Oh God!

O-words you'd like to add:

_____

_____

P IS FOR PLAY

Remember how life was when you didn't feel you had to be responsible for the well-being of the whole planet? Remember how goofy you felt when you first fell in love? Remember when sex felt erotic, exotic, clear, sharp, powerful, strong, natural, psychic, beautiful, and entirely "tuned in?"

- How goofy can you get?
- What tunes you in?

Other P-words to consider: Permission, Praise, Pleasure, Power, Partner, Passion, Promise, Pillow-talk, Penis, Petting, Porn, Pansexual, Penetration, Preference, Polyamory.

P-words you'd like to add:

_____

_____

Q IS FOR QUEST

Our sexual journeys are complex and varied and may lead us in directions we never expected when we started out. What are we looking for? Excitement? Satisfaction? Love? We may never know until suddenly there it is filling our energy field. The important thing is to engage in the journey. Take the first step, and then keep on keeping on.

- What erotic quest are you on?
- What have you found along the way?

Other Q-words to consider: Quirky, Quiet, Questioning, Quixotic, Quality, Quantum, Quivering, Queer, Queen.

Q-words you'd like to add:

_____

_____

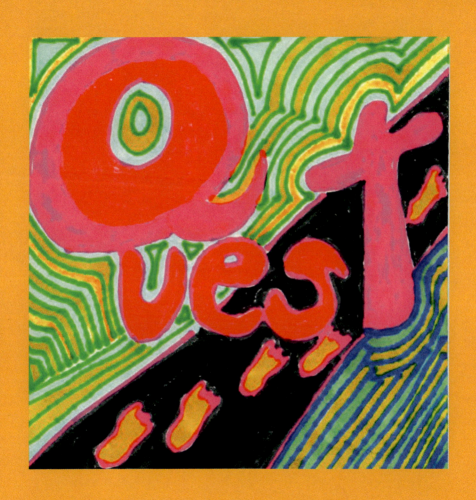

R IS FOR RELEASE

Before beginnings there have to be endings, Sexual release means letting go in every way—physical, emotional, mental, and spiritual. True release can feel like an orgasm of body and soul.

- What are you holding on to?
- What are you ready to let go of?

Other R-words to consider: Reaching, Racy, Ravishing, Romance, Recreation, Rigid, Ready, Relaxed, Rights, Rapture, Ritual, Relationship.

R-words you'd like to add:

_____

_____

S IS FOR SENSES

It's through our senses that we know who we are. It's through our senses that we locate ourselves in our world and in our relationships. Some say it's through our senses that we know God. In that way, sex can be a path to the soul.

- What feels good to you?
- How do you know who you are?

Other S-words to consider: Spirit, Soul, Sacred, Subtle, Skin hunger, Swinging, Sweaty, Shower, Slippery, Scent, Surprise, Spontaneous, Smell, Sigh, Synchronicity, Sleazy, Safety, Sexy, Self, Self-Esteem, Shag, Surrender, Sweetness, Seduce, Share, Sugar, Shakti, Shiva.

S-words you'd like to add:

_____

_____

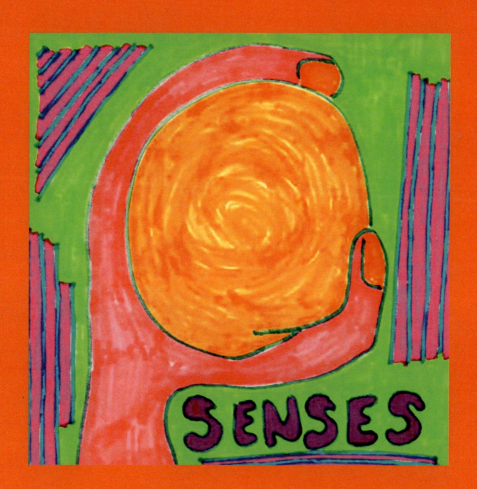

T IS FOR TOUCH

Laying on of hands is one of the most ancient forms of healing, blessing, and giving sexual pleasure—and not just "down there." Consider massage, consider all-over stroking or a neck rub, or nuzzling an ear lobe. One woman said, "I don't know where on my body I'm not orgasmic. I think I need to be mapped."

- How do you like to offer sensual, sexual touch?
- What are some of your favorite erogenous zones?

Other T-words to consider: Taste, Tongue, Tease, Tempt, Tart, Tummy, Tantalize, Tickle, Treat, Toys, Toes, Torrid, Tantra, Talk, Try, Trans, Transformation, Timeless.

T-words you'd like to add:

_____

_____

U IS FOR UP

Up is buoyancy. Up is transcendence. Up is when we feel transported to other realms by pleasure, orgasm, and ecstasy.

- How do you get to up?
- How do you come back to earth?

Other U-words to consider: Unique, Uppity, Understanding, Untamed, Unbuttoned, Urge, Undressed, Undulate, Ululate, Unusual, Urgent, Undies.

U-words you'd like to add:

_____

_____

V IS FOR VITAL

Vitality is the pulsing energy that makes us want to laugh, dance, sing, and maybe eat, love, and pray. The wonderful Welsh poet Dylan Thomas called it "the force that through the green fuse drives the flower."

- What lights your sexual fuse?
- What makes you want to sing?

Other V-words to consider: Vulva, Vagina, Vibrator, Viagra, Virility, Vanity, Vision, Variety, Voluptuous, Voracious, Vanilla, Velvet, Voice, Vivacious, Vixen.

V-words you'd like to add:

_____

_____

W IS FOR WONDER

There's so much more to love and sex than scientists are able to count and measure. Transpersonal psychiatrist Carl Jung called these the "irrational facts of experience."

- What is most wondrous to you about love?
- What is most wondrous to you about sex?

Other W-words to consider: Wild, Woman, Want, Whisper, Wish, Wank, Wine, Worship, Warm, Wow, We, Wheee!

W-words you'd like to add:

_____

_____

X IS FOR X-RATED

Sometimes what does it for us is sex that's off-beat, down-beat, down-to-earth, down-and-dirty. There are so many choices.

- What do you want?
- What's your "safe" word?

Other X-words to consider: eXotic, eXclaim, eXtraordinary, eXcess, eXtreme, eXplore, eXhale, eXuberant, eXtragenital, eXultant, Xoxoxoxo.

X-words you'd like to add:

_____

_____

Y IS FOR YES!

Yes is about exercising our own power—the power to move, the power to love, the power to feel.

- What are you ready to say Yes to?
- What makes you feel most powerful as a lover?

Other Y-words to consider: You, Yearn, Yin, Yang, Yoni, Yummy.

Y-words you'd like to add:

_____

_____

Z IS FOR ZONE

When we're in the Zone, we flow with self-esteem, confidence, connection, and a euphoric sense of how to give and receive delicious pleasure.

- How do you feel when you're in the Zone?
- What's your favorite way to get there?

Other Z-words to consider: Zipper, Zany, Zest, and its opposite Zzzzzzzzzzzzz.... And so good night!

Z-words you'd like to add:

_____

_____

APPRECIATIONS

To Jo Chaffee—for her thorough knowledge of the Alphabet.

To Belinda Morse—for creating the original book design--PDQ.

To Sue Katz—for addressing so many publishing QAs.

To Michele Stohen—for putting it all together at last—A to Z.

And most of all, appreciation for the life of Dr. Jane Claypool, teacher, minister, prolific author, and dear friend, who left her body in 2014, before she could see this book published.

Information in this book is grounded in nuances of the 4-Dimensional Wheel approach to sexual experience. For more information please see both my websites: GinaOgden.com and 4-DNetwork.com.

I welcome your questions and comments!
Please address all inquiries about this book to me:
Gina Ogden, founder of the 4-D Network for Body, Mind, Heart, and Spirit:
Gina@4-DNetwork.com

Made in the USA
Middletown, DE
17 July 2019